ANGER MANAGEMENT AND YOU

**Life Skills Series
Basic Skills for Lifelong Success**

Please read:

Talk to your health-care provider! This workbook is not a substitute for the advice of a qualified health-care provider.

Reentry Essentials, Inc.
98 4th Street, Suite 414
Brooklyn, NY 11231
P: 347.973.0004
E: info@ReentryEssentials.org
I: www.ReentryEssentials.org

© 2019. Reentry Essentials, Inc. All rights reserved. No part of the material protected by this copyright may be reproduced or used in any form or by any means, electronic or mechanical, including photocopying, recording or by information storage and retrieval system without written permission from the copyright owner.

This workbook belongs to:

_____

You may find it helpful to keep important names and phone numbers handy.

Write them below.

Health-care provider

Name_____

Phone_____

Counselor

Name_____

Phone_____

Emergency contact

Name_____

Phone_____

Other important numbers

Name_____

Phone_____

Other important numbers

_____
_____
_____
_____
_____
_____
_____
_____
_____
_____
_____
_____
_____
_____
_____

THIS WORKBOOK CAN HELP YOU MANAGE YOUR ANGER.

It can help you understand what causes your anger and the problems that can result if you're unable to control it. It will also help you learn ways to manage and express your anger.

Anger is a powerful feeling.

Everyone feels angry sometimes. And everyone has a right to feel that way. It's what you do with your anger that makes the difference.

Managing your anger appropriately is an important skill.

It involves:

- identifying what triggers your anger
- learning how to calm yourself
- finding healthy ways to express your anger without losing control and hurting yourself or others

CONTENT

What is anger? 3
What causes anger? 4
Poorly handled anger can cause many problems. 5
Uncontrolled anger can lead to aggression. 7
How anger can help you 8
Is your anger hurting you? 9
Recognizing your body's anger warning signs 11
What sets you off? 12
Keep an "anger journal." 13
Be aware of hidden anger. 15
Some reactions to anger won't help. 16
Using alcohol or other drugs only causes more problems. 17
Take steps to get back control 18
Find healthy ways to express your anger. 19
Practice using "I" statements. 20
How do you talk to yourself? 21
Practice your positive self-talk. 22
Physical activity is a great outlet for angry feelings. 23
More ways to help get a handle on anger 24
Learning to relax can help you stay on control 25
Dealing with someone else's anger 27
Sources of help 28
Develop an anger management plan. 29
My anger management plan 30

WHAT IS ANGER?
Anger is a natural emotional reaction.

Anger affects your body.

When you get angry, your body creates energy. Here's what happens:

- Adrenaline and other chemicals enter your bloodstream.
- Your heart pumps faster.
- Your blood flows more quickly.
- Your muscles tense.

Everyone gets angry sometimes.

Handling anger well can help you:

- overcome problems
- reach your goals
- stay healthy
- feel better about yourself

But too much anger or uncontrolled anger can cause problems.

It can cause:

- problems in your relationships with family and friends
- problems at work
- legal and financial troubles
- physical and mental health problems

How can you tell when you are getting angry?

_____
_____
_____
_____
_____
_____
_____
_____
_____
_____
_____
_____
_____
_____
_____
_____
_____
_____
_____

Anger isn't good or bad. It's what you do with it that counts.

WHAT CAUSES ANGER?

The causes vary from person to person and from situation to situation. Some common causes of anger include:

Stress

Stress related to work, family, health and money problems may make you feel anxious and irritable.

Frustration

You may get angry if you fail to reach a goal or feel as if things are out of your control.

Fear

Anger is a natural response to threats of violence, or to physical or verbal abuse.

Annoyance

You may react in anger to minor irritations and daily hassles.

Disappointment

Anger often results when expectations and desires aren't met.

Resentment

You may feel angry when you've been hurt, rejected or offended.

Think about a time you got angry due to one of the causes listed on this page. What was it that made you angry? Write about it here:

_____
_____
_____
_____
_____
_____
_____
_____
_____
_____
_____
_____
_____
_____
_____
_____
_____
_____
_____
_____
_____
_____
_____
_____

POORLY HANDLED ANGER CAN CAUSE MANY PROBLEMS.
Some people try to pretend they aren't angry. Other people feel as if their anger is out of control. They don't believe they can handle it. But ignoring or giving up control over it can lead to:

Physical health problems

These may include:

- headaches
- sleep problems
- digestive problems
- high blood pressure
- heart problems

Poor decision making

Anger can make it hard to think clearly. You may have trouble concentrating or may use poor judgment. This can lead to car crashes, injuries and other problems.

Problems with relationships

If you can't control your anger, you may end up insulting, criticizing or threatening those close to you. They may respond with anger or resentment. Getting angry may also keep you from telling your loved ones how you really feel.

Depression

Anger that's kept bottled up can affect your thoughts and feelings. You may begin to feel unhappy and lose interest in things you used to enjoy, such as hobbies, work, friends or sex.

Alcohol or other drug problems

You may use alcohol or other drugs to try to:

- dull anger and other strong feelings
- forget about the negative consequences of an angry outburst

But using alcohol or other drugs won't solve any problems. And it usually results in more anger and problems.

Low self-esteem

If you have trouble managing anger, you may feel bad about yourself. You may feel as if you have little control over what happens.

Problems at work

If you blow up on the job, coworkers, supervisors, and customers may develop a negative impression of you. Your career may suffer as a result.

Learning how to keep your cool can help you lead a happier, healthier life.

Has anger ever caused problems for you? Write about it here:

_____
_____
_____
_____
_____
_____
_____
_____
_____
_____
_____
_____
_____
_____

UNCONTROLLED ANGER CAN LEAD TO AGGRESSION.

The results of uncontrolled anger may include:

Verbal attacks or physical assaults

You may lose control and attack others physically or verbally.

For example, you may:

- throw or break things
- yell, insult or threaten
- slap, shove, kick or hit

Abuse

Tension and frustration may build. Family members may become your target, even if your anger has little to do with them. The abuse may be:

- physical
- verbal
- sexual

Other criminal behavior

Anger is often a driving force behind:

- destruction of property
- murder
- other violent crimes

But remember, you can learn to control your anger.

HOW ANGER CAN HELP YOU

Learning to recognize and express anger appropriately can make a big difference in your life. Anger can help you:

Reach goals

Trying to reach a goal can be frustrating. Frustration can lead to anger, which in turn can motivate you to work harder.

Solve problems

Anger is a sign that something is wrong. It may serve as a warning for you to think about your feelings and attitudes.

Handle emergencies and protect yourself

Anger can cause an immediate burst of strength and energy. This allows you to react quickly if you're in danger.

Communicate with others

Talking about your anger can help keep it from building up. You may release tension and enjoy better communication with family, friends and co-workers.

You can find ways to help anger work for you - not against you.

IS YOUR ANGER HURTING YOU?

Think about how often you get angry and how you handle angry feelings. Complete the checklist below. It can help you decide if you need help managing your anger.

Am I prone to anger?	True	False
1. I feel tense a lot of the time.	☐	☐
2. People often tell me I need to calm down.	☐	☐
3. I get angry quickly.	☐	☐
4. I stay angry for a long time.	☐	☐
5. Sometimes it seems like everything makes me angry.	☐	☐
6. Minor troubles annoy me more than they do most people.	☐	☐
7. I often blame my troubles on other people.	☐	☐
8. When I feel wronged, I want revenge.	☐	☐
9. Getting angry makes me feel powerful and in control.	☐	☐
10. I am still angry about bad things that happened to me in the past.	☐	☐
11. I get into a lot of arguments.	☐	☐
12. I get very upset when things don't go my way.	☐	☐

If you answered "true" to any question above, you may get angry more often than most people.

Too much anger can cause problems in your life. But you can take steps to reduce the amount of anger you feel.

How do I handle my anger?	True	False
1. I store up anger until I'm about to explode	☐	☐
2. I try to ignore my anger in the hope it will go away	☐	☐
3. When angry, I say or do things that I later regret	☐	☐
4. My anger:		
• frightens me	☐	☐
• frightens others	☐	☐
5. When I get angry, I:		
• yell or scream	☐	☐
• cry uncontrollably	☐	☐
• break things	☐	☐
• hurt myself	☐	☐
• hurt others (physically and/or verbally)	☐	☐
6. My anger has resulted in:		
• problems at work or school	☐	☐
• problems at home	☐	☐
• trouble with the law	☐	☐
7. I have tried to control my anger and failed	☐	☐
8. I use alcohol or other drugs to try to cover up angry feelings	☐	☐
9. I sometimes feel out of control when I'm angry	☐	☐
10. I want help managing my anger	☐	☐

If you answered "true" to any question above, you may have trouble handling your anger.

You can learn ways to keep your cool and stay in control when you get angry.

RECOGNIZING YOUR BODY'S ANGER WARNING SIGNS
is an important step in learning to manage your anger.

What are your warning signs?

Think about how you feel when you get angry. Check the warning signs you often have when you get angry. Write in signs that aren't listed.

My warning signs are:

- ☐ tense muscles
- ☐ tight fists
- ☐ clenched jaw
- ☐ sweaty palms
- ☐ racing heartbeat
- ☐ fast breathing
- ☐ trembling or feeling shaky
- ☐ feeling warm or flushed
- ☐ upset stomach
- ☐ loud or mean voice
- ☐ _____
- ☐ _____
- ☐ _____
- ☐ _____
- ☐ _____
- ☐ _____
- ☐ _____
- ☐ _____

Talk with your health-care provider.

Certain physical and mental health problems, such as Alzheimer's disease or brain injury, may increase your anger. And handling anger poorly can lead to other health problems. Talk to your healthcare provider about your anger and how it affects you. Have regular checkups.

WHAT SETS YOU OFF?

Different things can trigger a person's anger. Some common triggers are listed below. Check the ones that trigger your anger. Use the blank spaces to fill in your own triggers.

I feel angry when I:
- ☐ think I am treated unfairly
- ☐ am embarrassed
- ☐ feel ignored
- ☐ don't get credit for something I've done
- ☐ have to follow orders
- ☐ fail at something or don't do something well
- ☐ feel helpless or out of control
- ☐ get jealous
- ☐ _____
- ☐ _____
- ☐ _____
- ☐ _____
- ☐ _____
- ☐ _____

I feel angry when people:
- ☐ insult me
- ☐ criticize me or my work
- ☐ don't listen to me
- ☐ disagree with me
- ☐ don't work as hard as I do
- ☐ lie to me
- ☐ tell me what to do
- ☐ are rude or inconsiderate
- ☐ are late
- ☐ don't act or feel the way I think they should
- ☐ _____
- ☐ _____
- ☐ _____
- ☐ _____
- ☐ _____
- ☐ _____

I feel angry when faced with these events or situations:
- ☐ traffic jams and encounters with other drivers
- ☐ conflict at work
- ☐ family arguments
- ☐ child misbehavior or temper tantrums
- ☐ waiting in line
- ☐ financial problems
- ☐ yelling or loud noises
- ☐ mistakes or errors
- ☐ wasted time
- ☐ losing a game or a contest
- ☐ name-calling or teasing
- ☐ child abuse
- ☐ prejudice toward anyone
- ☐ mistreatment of animals
- ☐ _____
- ☐ _____
- ☐ _____
- ☐ _____
- ☐ _____

Once you're aware of your anger triggers, you can work to change the way you respond to them.

KEEP AN "ANGER JOURNAL".

Use these 2 pages to start your journal.
Over the next several days, keep track of things that trigger your anger.

Date and Time	Trigger	My Anger Warning Signs	My Anger Rating 1 = mild 2 = moderate 3 = severe	What I Did In Response	How I Felt Afterwards

Do you notice patterns in your anger? For example, do minor triggers often set you off? Does your anger rating seem out of proportion to the trigger? Are you satisfied with the outcome?

Date and Time	Trigger	My Anger Warning Signs	My Anger Rating 1 = mild 2 = moderate 3 = severe	What I Did In Response	How I Felt Afterwards

BE AWARE OF HIDDEN ANGER.

Sometimes what triggers your anger isn't the only thing causing angry feeling. When you get angry, ask yourself:

Are my level of anger and my reaction out of proportion to the trigger?

Do you seem to overreact to minor annoyances? Perhaps there is something else on your mind that's making you angry.

Am I directing my anger at an innocent person?

Are really angry with the person who triggered your feelings? For example, suppose you have a disagreement with your boss. It bothers you all day, but you say nothing. Later, you let your anger out by blowing up at your partner or child.

Am I taking something personally?

Learning to deal well anger means learning not to take problems or arguments personally.

Is this how I usually respond in similar situations?

You may respond with anger in certain situations because that's what you've always done. You may have learned this behavior growing up. But you can change the way you react.

Am I trying to take charge with my anger?

Anger is a common reaction when a person feels as if he or she is losing control. But the best way to show control is to react calmly and manage your feelings.

SOME REACTIONS TO ANGER WON'T HELP.

Many people react poorly to anger. Their reaction doesn't help them control their anger. And sometimes their reaction can make things worse. Avoid negative reactions, such as:

Not letting go

You may have trouble getting past your anger. You may remember events or hurts that occurred long ago. As time goes by, your anger may continue to grow. You may become obsessed with angry thoughts or hopes of revenge.

Keeping bottled up

This usually makes you feel worse. Sooner or later, your feelings will come out. And when they do, it may be in the form of an angry outburst. Holding angry feelings in may also contribute to health problems.

Blaming

Blaming others doesn't solve problems. You need to learn to take responsibility for your own feelings and actions— both positive and negative.

Responding to anger with anger

This may seem like a natural reaction, but it often makes a situation worse.

Think about a time you did not handle anger well. What happened?

Write about it here:

_____
_____
_____
_____
_____
_____
_____
_____
_____
_____
_____
_____
_____
_____
_____
_____
_____
_____
_____
_____
_____
_____
_____
_____

USING ALCOHOL OR OTHER DRUGS ONLY CAUSES MORE PROBLEMS.

They do little to get rid of angry feelings. They can make it harder for you to think clearly and solve problems. It's important to know that:

Alcohol or other drug use may increase anger.

Using alcohol or other drugs to dull anger doesn't work. These substances may mask angry feelings—but only for a short time. And they often make anger worse. Alcohol and other drugs play a major role in many cases of violence.

You shouldn't use alcohol or other drugs as an excuse for angry or violent behavior.

The truth is, there's no excuse for losing control in this way.

Treatment programs are available.

Some treatment programs are designed to help people recover from an alcohol or drug problem and learn to manage their anger.

Get help if you have a problem with alcohol or other drugs.

- Call the Center for Substance Abuse Treatment's National Helpline at

    1-800-662-HELP
    (1-800-662-4357)

- Look in the phone book for numbers of local self-help groups, such as Alcoholics Anonymous (AA).

Having a problem with alcohol or other drugs makes it harder to manage anger.

Look in the phone book for local sources of help for substance abuse.

Write down their contact information here:

Name_____

_____

Phone number_____

Name_____

_____

Phone number_____

Name_____

_____

Phone number_____

TAKE STEPS TO GET BACK CONTROL
When you're angry. Start by taking a "timeout":

Stop what you're doing

When you feel your anger warning signs developing and you start thinking angry thoughts, tell yourself to stop. This may help you calm down and think more clearly.

Try to relax

For example:

- Count to 10 or 100.
- Get a drink of water.
- Take a walk.
- Take several slow, deep breaths.

Leave if necessary

If you are angry with another person, tell him or her that you need to take a timeout. Ask someone to watch a child or an elderly or ill person for you, if necessary. Then go for a walk and calm down. Avoid driving.

Return when your calm

Once you've got your anger under control, go back and talk with the person or face the situation that triggered your anger.

Think about a time when you didn't lose control of your anger and handled it well.

What happened? Write about it here:

_____
_____
_____
_____
_____
_____
_____
_____
_____
_____
_____
_____
_____
_____
_____
_____
_____
_____
_____
_____

FIND HEALTHY WAYS TO EXPRESS YOUR ANGER.

Don't keep angry feelings locked inside you. Express them in ways that help you keep control—and won't hurt others.

Remember to calm down.

Think carefully before you speak. You're less likely to say something you'll be sorry for later.

Name the problem.

Calmly and clearly explain why you're angry or what the problem is. Don't yell, use insults or make threats. People will be less likely to consider your point.

Use "I" statements.

After you describe the problem use "I" statements to tell the person how you feel. These statements focus on you and your needs, wants and feelings. They also help the listener avoid feeling blamed or criticized. (See the next page for examples.)

Identify solutions.

Say what you would like to change or see happen in the future. If you're having a conflict with another person, try to find a solution together.

Get help if you need it.

Talk with a family member or friend if you're having trouble expressing your anger constructively. Or consider seeing a counselor or other mental health professional. He or she can help you learn ways to express your feelings through role-playing and other methods. (See page 28.)

Don't hold a grudge. After a disagreement, be willing to forgive the other person— and yourself.

PRACTICE USING "I" STATEMENTS.

When you're angry, it's easy to blame someone or something for your problems. Getting comfortable using "I" statements can help you learn to take responsibility for your feelings. Fill in the statements below to practice talking in terms of yourself and your feelings.

I feel _____

When _____

Next time I would like

_____
_____
_____
_____
_____
_____

I feel _____

When _____

Next time I would like

_____
_____
_____
_____
_____
_____

I feel _____

When _____

Next time I would like

_____
_____
_____
_____
_____
_____

I feel _____

When _____

Next time I would like

_____
_____
_____
_____
_____
_____

I feel _____

When _____

Next time I would like

_____
_____
_____
_____
_____
_____

I feel _____

When _____

Next time I would like

_____
_____
_____
_____
_____
_____

HOW DO YOU TALK TO YOURSELF?

You may say things silently to yourself every day. This is called self-talk.

Avoid negative self-talk.

This includes criticizing yourself and blaming yourself or others for your problems. Negative self-talk can add to your anger and make it harder to manage.

Learn to use positive self-talk instead.

Try to stop negative self-talk as soon as it pops into your head. Replace the negative thought with a positive one. For example:

- Instead of saying, "I can't handle this traffic. I'm going to explode," you could say, "Relax. I can handle it. This happens to everyone sometimes. It won't last long."
- Instead of saying, "That jerk, she embarrassed me on purpose," you could say, "It's OK she probably didn't mean anything by it. Maybe she's just having a bad day."

Learning to identify negative messages and change them to positive ones can help reduce the amount of anger you feel

PRACTICE YOUR POSITIVE SELF-TALK.

In the space below, write down several problems or situations that made you angry. Did you give yourself a negative message? What positive message could you give yourself if the problem or situation happens again?

Situation	Negative Message	Positive Message
1. _____	_____	_____
_____	_____	_____
_____	_____	_____
2. _____	_____	_____
_____	_____	_____
_____	_____	_____
3. _____	_____	_____
_____	_____	_____
_____	_____	_____
4. _____	_____	_____
_____	_____	_____
_____	_____	_____
5. _____	_____	_____
_____	_____	_____
_____	_____	_____
6. _____	_____	_____
_____	_____	_____
_____	_____	_____

With time, it will get easier to replace your negative messages with positive ones. You may even find that you automatically think of positive messages.

PHYSICAL ACTIVITY IS A GREAT OUTLET FOR ANGRY FEELINGS.
It lets you quickly and safely let out strong feelings. And regular activity can improve your overall health. Here are some tips:

Talk with your healthcare provider.
Be sure to consult your healthcare provider before starting an exercise program.

Choose moderate activities.
Good choices include:
- walking
- swimming
- tennis
- dancing
- yoga

Just about any activity—even household chores—can be an effective outlet for your anger.

Don't overdo it.
Slowly increase the amount of activity you do. And be sure to warm up before you begin and cool down afterward.

What activities will you try to help manage you anger?
Write them here.
_____
_____
_____
_____
_____
_____
_____
_____
_____
_____
_____
_____
_____
_____
_____
_____
_____
_____
_____
_____
_____
_____
_____

MORE WAYS TO HELP GET A HANDLE ON ANGER.
When things start heating up, try these methods to cool down:

Have a sense of humor.

For many people, having a good sense of humor helps them avoid getting angry. Try to find the humor in minor troubles and annoyances.

Do a hobby.

For example, try gardening, learning a musical instrument or making crafts. A hobby can be a productive outlet for tension and energy. And it can serve as a welcome distraction from angry feelings.

Write about your feelings.

Consider recording your thoughts and feelings in a journal or diary. Or write a letter. (You don't have to send it.) Writing can help you work through situations and problems calmly and at your own pace.

Get plenty of rest

Most people need about 6-9 hours of sleep each day: When you're angry, you may have trouble falling asleep. In turn, this lack of sleep may leave you telling more irritable. If you have trouble sleeping:

- Go to bed at the same time each night.
- Avoid having caffeine at least 8 hours before going to bed. It can keep you awake.

LEARNING TO RELAX CAN HELP YOU STAY ON CONTROL.
Using relaxation techniques regularly can help you reduce stress and stay calm.

Meditation

This can help calm you and clear your mind of anger. Follow these steps:

1. Find a quiet place. Wear loose, comfortable clothing. Sit or lie down.
2. Close your eyes. Take slow, deep breaths.
3. Concentrate on a single word, object or calming thought.
4. Don't worry if other thoughts or images enter your mind while you are doing this. Just relax and return to what you were focusing on.
5. Continue until you feel relaxed and refreshed.

Deep-breathing exercises

These can help keep anger from getting out of control. Follow these steps:

1. Sit comfortably or lie on your back.
2. Breathe in slowly and deeply for a count of 5.
3. Hold your breath for a count of 5.
4. Breathe out slowly for a count of 5, pushing out all the air.
5. Repeat several times until you feel calm and relaxed.

Progressive muscle relaxation

Tense and relax each muscle group, starting at your head and working your way down to your toes. Here's how:

1. Wear loose, comfortable clothing. Sit in a comfortable chair or lie down.
2. Tense the muscles in your face for 5-10 seconds. Then relax them for about 20 seconds.
3. Tense the muscles in the back of your neck for 5-10 seconds. Then relax them for about 20 seconds. Notice the difference in how your muscles feel when relaxed.
4. Move down to your shoulders. Tense and relax the muscles the same way you did in step 3.
5. Repeat the same steps with the other muscle groups in your body—in your hands, arms, chest, stomach, lower back, buttocks, thighs, calves and feet—one at a time.

Visualization

This technique uses your imagination to help you relax and reduce your anger.

1. Sit in a comfortable chair or lie down.
2. Imagine a pleasant, peaceful scene, such as a lush forest or a sandy beach. Picture yourself in this setting.
3. Focus on the scene. Continue until you feel refreshed and relaxed.

Make an appointment to relax.

Write down a relaxation technique you'd like to try, then schedule a time when you can try it during the next week

Relaxation technique:
_____
_____
_____
_____
_____
_____

When I can try it:
_____
_____
_____
_____
_____
_____
_____
_____
_____
_____

Your health-care provider or local library can provide more information on these and other relaxation techniques.

DEALING WITH SOMEONE ELSE'S ANGER
Here are some tips:

Keep your cool.
Don't answer anger with anger. Remember that anger can lead people to say things they don't really mean. Criticism, threats or name-calling won't help resolve the situation.

Don't take it personally.
Try to understand why the person is angry. His or her feelings may have little or nothing to do with you.

Listen to the person.
Sometimes an angry person just needs to "blow off steam." Let the person express his or her feelings. Don't interrupt. Maintain eye contact to show you are listening.

Think of solutions together.
If you're having a conflict with someone, try to find solutions that you can both agree on. Do this only when you are both calm.

Don't take chances.
- If you're worried about your safety, get help right away. Try to leave yourself an escape path.
- If the person has a weapon, seek safety at the first opportunity. Don't confront or try to restrain him or her.

SOURCES OF HELP

You don't have to face your problems alone. Let others know that you want help controlling your anger. They can provide valuable support and encouragement. Consider contacting:

Your health-care provider

Your health-care provider can give you a physical exam and suggest relaxation techniques. He or she may also prescribe medications for related health conditions.

Mental health professionals and mental health centers

These provide a variety of services, including outpatient treatment and support groups.

Counselors, family therapists or social workers

They can help you learn ways to manage anger, control stress and solve problems.

Hotlines

Hotlines may provide emergency counseling to help you control angry feelings or behavior. Check your local phone book.

Employee Assistance Programs (EAPs)

These may offer referrals or counseling to help employees deal with issues like alcohol or other drug problems, job stress and relationship problems.

Religious leaders

They may offer advice and reassurance—or just listen when you need someone to talk to.

Asking for help is a sign of strength—not weakness.

DEVELOP AN ANGER MANAGEMENT PLAN.

Now that you've learned more about anger and how you respond to it, you can develop your own plan for managing your anger. Follow these steps:

1. Set positive goals and a time frame.

Your goals should address both a specific behavior and your reaction. For example, over the next month, your goal could be to communicate your feelings using "I" statements whenever you get angry at work.

You can set different goals for yourself. But don't try to meet too many at one time. You're less likely to reach them.

2. Get support.

Tell family, friends and coworkers about your goals. They can offer encouragement and advice. Seek out their help if you're having trouble with your anger. Or consider seeing a mental health professional.

3. Track your progress.

Consider keeping a daily log or journal. Make note of times when you avoid getting angry or handle anger well. Seeing improvement over time can keep you from feeling discouraged.

4. Reward yourself.

Treat yourself when you reach a goal or get halfway there. For example, go to a movie or enjoy a special meal.

MY ANGER MANAGEMENT PLAN

Goal:

_____
_____
_____
_____

My action plan:

_____
_____
_____
_____

Target date:

_____
_____
_____
_____

Reward:

_____
_____
_____
_____

People I can call one for help:

_____
_____
_____
_____

Learning to manage your anger takes time and effort. But you'll find the results are worth it

Made in the USA
Columbia, SC
14 October 2024

43666955R00020